"This poetic commentary weaves biblical narrative with contemporary issues of justice, lament, and hope. It is for anyone looking to meditate deeply on the Gospels. Jackson's unique approach, along with his heart for God's Word, makes this collection an instant classic, a true gift to the church."

Rachel Joy Welcher, editor at *Fathom Magazine* and author of *Talking Back to Purity Culture: Rediscovering Faithful Christian Sexuality*

"If poetry is the art of the indirect, the undefended doorway into deeper consciousness, then Drew Jackson is a wonderful new teacher on the scene! Seldom have I read such direct insight into spiritual moments and spiritual matters. . . . I am already eager to see and hear more!"

Richard Rohr, Center for Action and Contemplation

"With undeniable depth and brilliant creativity, Drew Jackson offers a powerful poetic tour through the Gospel of Luke. Drew joins poignant cultural analysis with biblical faithfulness, and does so in a way that kept me captivated throughout. This book is a gift, offering us a fresh vision of the gospel story with profound flow."

Rich Villodas, lead pastor of New Life Fellowship and author of *The Deeply Formed Life*

"*God Speaks Through Wombs* is a fresh take on the first eight chapters of the Gospel of Luke and a poetic invitation into the world of the Scriptures. What we read here is not translation, but rather more. We are transported into the ministry of Jesus and beckoned to walk alongside him with the oppressed he came to save. Jackson's poetry brings to light the fact that Christ's ministry is, in many ways, an affirmation of human dignity in general and of Black dignity specifically. This Savior is very much for you, not against you."

Malcolm B. Foley, director of the Black Church Studies Program at Truett Seminary

"This book of poetry offers a beautifully nuanced perspective on themes of oppression, of liberation, of suffering, of hope for what has been promised. Drew weaves together biblical experiences with the language and perspectives of modern activists. His poetry allows us to experience the voice of God through words on the page. I will be using these poems for creative inspiration, as prayer, as a liturgy for all the things that are difficult to speak about in a dark and difficult world. This collection will offer you great solace, speaking life into your spirit."

Nikole Lim, founder and international director of Freely in Hope and author of *Liberation Is Here*

"I've known Drew for over a decade, and this book bears witness to his soul: a careful listener, passionate conversation partner, bold truth teller, and tenderhearted empath. Drew has always been an artist, crafty with words and sounds. *God Speaks Through Wombs* reflects Drew's soulful artistry. Through his poetic genius, Drew effortlessly weaves together the ancient stories of the Gospel of Luke with social movement history, popular culture, contemporary justice issues, theological rigor, and more. Every pastor, theologian, faith-rooted activist, and person of faith who cares about the intersection of faith and justice needs this book. You won't be able to preach, teach, pray, sing, or question the Gospel of Luke the same!"

Brandon Wrencher, organizer, writer, and founding pastor of the
Good Neighbor Movement

Foreword by Jon Batiste

GOD SPEAKS THROUGH WOMBS

Poems on God's Unexpected Coming

Drew Jackson

An imprint of InterVarsity Press
Downers Grove, Illinois

InterVarsity Press
P.O. Box 1400, Downers Grove, IL 60515-1426
ivpress.com
email@ivpress.com

InterVarsity Press® is the book-publishing division of InterVarsity Christian Fellowship/USA®, a movement of
students and faculty active on campus at hundreds of universities, colleges, and schools of nursing in the United
States of America, and a member movement of the International Fellowship of Evangelical Students. For
information about local and regional activities, visit intervarsity.org.

While any stories in this book are true, some names and identifying information may have been changed to
protect the privacy of individuals.

Cover design and image composite: David Fassett
Interior design: Daniel van Loon
Images: smooth white paper: © Nenov / Moment Collection / Getty Images
     open Bible: © "Design, Pics" / Getty Images
     abstract star-shaped painting: © beastfromeast / DigitalVision Vectors / Getty Images

ISBN 978-1-5140-0267-4 (print)
ISBN 978-1-5140-0268-1 (digital)

Library of Congress Cataloging-in-Publication Data
A catalog record for this book is available from the Library of Congress.

P 25 24 23 22 21 20 19 18 17 16 15 14 13 12 11 10 9 8 7 6 5 4 3 2 1

Y 42 41 40 39 38 37 36 35 34 33 32 31 30 29 28 27 26 25 24 23 22 21

FOR GENAY, MOM, ZORA & SUHAILA

The women who have been mouthpieces of God in my life

• • •

In memory of

DEBRA ELEASE JACKSON

(1956–2013)

Nobody's free until everybody's free.
FANNIE LOU HAMER

We are each other's harvest; we are each other's business;
we are each other's magnitude and bond.
GWENDOLYN BROOKS

We cannot create what we can't imagine.
LUCILLE CLIFTON

Contents

IV. Temptations

V. Rolling Deep

VI. On the Plain

VII. Life Lessons

VIII. Parables and Other Things

Foreword

Jon Batiste

The creative process is mysterious. It calls us to create meaning and value on a blank canvas, to translate the invisible, all-knowing language of God into poetic, universal prose.

The joy and pain of our lives can leave us speechless. This is partly why we feel compelled to join our life experiences—those past, present, and future—with others through the embrace of creativity. Whether in the form of encouragement, edification, exhalation, or exasperation, it is human to create art that documents our time on earth. For some of us this is a major part of our calling. Which brings me to why the artistic contributions of brother Drew Jackson's artful words are so important.

One of many things that inspire me about Drew is the way he is using his time on earth. He'll craft a sermon that might voyage through centuries of world history with scholarly scriptural accuracy, all while maintaining a crystal clear, Spirit-led, down-home message that welcomes you even as it challenges you. He finds a way to compassionately address a range of humanity, weaving in anecdotes from his personal narrative, without forsaking any aspect of the gospel. Just from hearing his sermons you know that he is in touch with his divine creative gift. This book is an extension of that gift.

Drew is led by the example of Christ and strives to walk in the footsteps of the great followers of God. In the words of Martin Luther King Jr., one of Drew's greatest inspirations, "We must use time creatively, in the knowledge that the time is always ripe to do right." In a time like this, we need divine creativity, and the words Drew has written are just that.

I have sat with Drew many times, absorbing his words as we worship, communing with each other in fellowship over some good meals, or lamenting each other's losses, and he puts his whole self into the moment. His words are powerful, and his creative process is filled with mysterious and divine wonder that you will find to be meaningful for many years to come.

• • •

Jon Batiste is a Grammy-nominated musician living in New York City. He is the bandleader of Stay Human and appears with them nightly as bandleader and musical director for The Late Show with Stephen Colbert. *He was co-composer (with Trent Reznor and Atticus Ross) for the Pixar film* Soul, *for which he received a Golden Globe, a BAFTA, and an Academy Award for Best Original Score.*

Introduction

There is a tradition, rooted in Jewish Midrashic thought, that understands the five books of the Psalter to be in conversation with the five books of Torah. Each book of Psalms is not meant to be a commentary on the corresponding book of Torah—the second book of Psalms doesn't walk verse by verse through Exodus—but the psalmists engage the themes of each book of Torah, pulling together words into beautiful poetic verse. When I read in Psalm 46:1, "God is our refuge and strength, a very present help in trouble," or Psalm 72:1, "Give the king your justice, O God, and your righteousness to the royal son" (ESV), I recognize that this poetry has been woven together by the strands of liberation and deliverance found in the book of Exodus. These are freedom songs, penned by those who experienced life from history's underside but who knew God to be a God committed to their liberation.

Before I began to write *God Speaks Through Wombs*, I asked myself what it might look like in our day if the liberative message of the Gospels gave birth to poetry. The message of God's activity in Jesus to deliver the world from injustice, oppression, and the bondage of death has been co-opted by those at the center of power, who have used it to carry out oppression. But Rome did not write the Scriptures—these words were given to us by those who knew the depths of poverty, who were constantly threatened by the brutality of policing forces, and who had to learn how to "sing the LORD's song in a foreign land" because they had been forcibly ripped from their own (Psalm 137:4 ESV). In thinking about this reality, I was drawn to the Gospel of Luke, since Luke is especially interested in showing us that the good news of the gospel is good news for the poor. And not only is this good news *for* the poor, but it must be heard *from* them as well.

....

I write these poems from my interest in the contours of biblical and theological discourse, and I also write unapologetically as a Black man—a Black man who moves through the world in a Black body and who knows from lived experience that not all who look upon my Black skin love it as I do. A Black man who has been formed by the work of Langston Hughes, Lucille Clifton, and Nas. A Black man who has been soothed by the sounds of John Coltrane and who has sat under the tutelage of a Black mother, born and bred in the Richard Allen projects of North Philly. These poems are not simply a commentary on Luke's words but an expression of my experience of Black love, Black longing, and Black joy.

I also write these poems as the son of a mother whose shadow never darkened a pulpit—she was told she was not allowed—but who taught me more about the liberating love of God than any pastor, priest, or professor. Though she is no longer with us, her words continue to resonate in my soul, and they have found their way onto these pages. She was a poet, from whom I inherited my love of words.

I am a poet, but I also believe that poetry gives us a way to "tell all the truth but tell it slant," as Emily Dickinson says. The Black faith and spirituality that has nourished me is steeped in the prophetic tradition, and it has always been compelling to me that the Hebrew prophets were poets. Isaiah, Jeremiah, and Amos were poets who spoke into their times out of a well of deep love. I believe that we need poetry in our time, as in every time, for the beauty it brings in the midst of brutality and also for its ability to cut into our hearts.

This collection of poems is a small contribution to a much larger conversation that has been happening for millennia—from journeys through the wilderness, to the hulls of slave ships, to the pews of Black churches, to Grandma's kitchen table. We have always known that liberation is God's prerogative and our inheritance as those made in the image of God, and we have used story, song, poetry, and prose to remind each other of this. Whether you have been privy to this conversation for a long time or are just sitting down at this table, I hope that these poems move you toward being swept up in the current of justice that has been flowing ever since God said "Let there be" (Genesis 1).

My hope is that *God Speaks Through Wombs* would be engaged by lovers of poetry as well as those who may be stepping into poetry for the first time. And although this collection is in conversation with the Gospel of Luke, it is not only meant for those who are well-versed in the Bible. These poems can be read alongside the corresponding passages of Scripture, but they can also stand alone. Poetry has always interacted with faith and spirituality because poetry invites us to explore our interior landscape. A poem invites us to slow down—in fact, it demands it—and it serves as a "gesture toward home," as the poet Jericho Brown says, welcoming us to return to our true dwelling place. Whoever you are, this book is for you.

As you read you may find yourself filled with righteous indignation, moved to silence, or even compelled to dance. Whatever it is, allow yourself to feel these words and to be caught up in the long struggle for freedom in which these poems found their shape.

I

OPENINGS

THEOPHILUS
(LOVER OF GOD)

Luke 1:1-4

History.
Told by those
lovers of Adonai
from the underside.

This story.
From the mouths
of the disempowered
and marginalized.

This account.
Transmitted
by handpicked
eyewitnesses.

These bodies.
Trampled
to the ground
by imperial power.

Have confidence
in what
you hear
from them.

GOD SPEAKS
THROUGH WOMBS

Luke 1:5-25

In the days of empires
and puppet regimes,
God speaks.

Through wombs,
wrested and discarded
because they were unviable.
This is what they do:
the Romes,
the Babylons,
the USAs,
the men—
toss to the side, as detritus,
what they've deemed unfit
to be utilized.

But God speaks through wombs,
birthing prophetic utterances.
The object of public scorn
given the power to name
the happenings of the Lord.
Elizabeth is her name.
Say her name.
It is she who will be
the one through whom
the covenant is kept.

She, like a priestess, speaks her word
while the leading male voices
are shut. Enough
of this unbelieving religion
that masquerades as faith.
Divine favor is placed
on what we have disgraced.

THE SPIRIT OF ELIJAH

Luke 1:14-18

I've been told that God shows up
on shores, in boats, with Bibles
and swords.

I've been told that God does
the bidding of kings
seeking to plant their flag on my soil.

I've been told that God snuggles up to
power that delights to
kill bodies like mine.

But that's not what Gabriel said.

Gabriel said that God's prophet
will have the spirit of Elijah,
bringing life to widows' households.

Gabriel said that God's prophet
will possess the power of the Tishbite,
tearing down monuments to the god of domination.

Gabriel said that God's prophet
will be filled with the Holy Spirit,
committed to speaking out against Ahabs and Jezebels.

Thus saith the LORD.

Nazareth

Luke 1:26

South central Galilee.
God comes to the southside.

Selah

Not to gentrify.
Not to church plant.
But to plant the seed
of righteous revolution.

Salvation is from the southside,
not from those
from the outside.

Selah

THEOTOKOS (GOD-BEARER)

Luke 1:26-38

Young. Brown.
From *that* side of town.
And now
with a baby
on the way.

You call her blessed?
I've heard her called worse things.

> *Thot*
> *Ho*
> *Bust-down*
> *Tramp*

No wonder she is troubled
by this greeting.
But they can't see
what You see.
What do they know?
She is holy.
Theotokos.

Overshadowed.
The Spirit hovers,
and she is covered.
Ready to birth
new creation.
Delivering us
salvation.

Say His Name

Luke 1:31-33

What did you say his name was?
I heard of him before.
Ain't that the little boy
who kicks it down by the corner store?

What was his name, you say?
Isn't that the homie
that used to live
around the way?

Say his name again?
Oh yeah,
that dude.
That's so and so's friend.

I swear, I know his name.
I thought he was the one
who got locked up
when the Feds came.

What's his name?
How could I forget. My bad.
He's the one whose name was trending,
preceded by a hashtag.

Everyone knows his name,
and make no mistake,
his momma always told us
her baby boy would be great.
#sayhisname

LEAP!

Luke 1:39-45

The dream
is no longer
deferred.

So we *leap*!
   We can't help it!

It rises up from within.
   From deep, guttural places.
      You can't contain our dance!

Feel the pit-pat!
   Hear the tip-tap!
      That's the rhythm of freedom.

Let the babies dance!
   Let them tell us of salvation.
      Let them lead us to liberation!

The babies are inviting us
   into the dance of a future
      on the threshold of birth.

And we will *leap!*
   We will *leap!*
      We will *leap!*

All the way there!

THAT GIRL CAN SING!

Luke 1:46-56

I mean, she can sang!
She has a voice
that can shatter shackles.
Her tune is no soothing lullaby;
it thunders down
through the arena of time.

   Sing, Mary! Sing!

Like Fannie at the marches.
Like the High Priestess of Soul
belting out her *Black Gold*.
Like Hannah breaking bows
of mighty warriors.

   You betta sing, Mary!

Watch out! The sound of her voice
will cast them down! Way down!
No doubt they will try to quiet you,
soften you, make you into
a domesticated maiden,
but we're gonna play this song.

   Go on, Mary!

Bless our ears with your sonic theology.
Lift us up with your melodic doctrine.
Magnify! Magnify!
This voice is magnificent.

HE'S NOT LIKE
HIS FATHER

Luke 1:57-66

She looks at his face on the eighth day:

This boy is different from his father. I
can see it in his eyes. His soft eyes
speak of infinite possibilities. It's silly,
but with his smile he seems to be
telling me not to believe only in the logical.
No, this boy is not like his father.

She squints her eyes at his tiny face:

He really doesn't look like a Zechariah.
He reminds me more of Uncle Elijah,
maybe Cousin Malachi, but different.
What is it? There's a determination
in his babyface. And there's so much grace.
So much grace all over him.
I think I'll call him John.

She looks at them, the ones puzzled at her choice:

Yes, I know his name is not the same
as the relatives. And I know,
this naming thing is delicate. But sometimes
you have to make a break in order to change
the trajectory of the story. And let me tell you,
this boy is going to change the game.
So remember the name.

Faith Opens Mouths

Luke 1:67-80

unclenches jaws
and minds
that could not
fathom

the chasm
between my hopes and
what's actually possible
being closed

because old dreams
don't resurrect or
sprout anew they
remain barren

where and when
they passed away
but faith opens
mouths

and grounds and
skies and wombs
and tombs and
hearts

to fresh starts
and fresh words
that speak of
things impossible

II

REVELATIONS

In Those (These) Days

Luke 2:1-3

Two things are certain,
three are guaranteed.

Death. Taxes. Empire.

The empire
will tax us
to death.

We will be dead
if we don't pay
the empire's taxes.

The empire
loves
taxes.

The empire
loves
death.

Of this
I am
certain.

O LITTLE TOWN

Luke 2:4-7

This city,
more like a little town,
has legacies of royal crowns.

This town,
closer to a village,
always and forever pillaged.

This village,
surrounded by settlements,
will boast of things heaven sent.

O little town
don't tear us down.
We need room to birth our children.

WHERE LAMBS FEED

Luke 2:6-7

This moment is singular.
A blank space.   A blank slate,

before the world has its chance
to mark you,
scar you
with harsh words.

What locution will I utter
as your initiation
into this world of
sentence and syllable?

I think I will sing again.
A lullaby this time.
And this is the lesson
I will teach you:

Even revolutionaries
must know when
the time is right
to sing softly.

Census Day

Luke 2:8-14

Under the canopy of this star-filled sky
there is much on our minds tonight.
We've heard the recent news: another census.
More than counting heads
they are counting dollars and cents.
Calculating how much they can extract from us again.

ROMAN EMPIRE CENSUS

DEPARTMENT OF COMMERCE

PLEASE ACCURATELY ANSWER THE FOLLOWING:

HOW MANY PEOPLE LIVE IN YOUR HOUSEHOLD?

WHAT IS YOUR OCCUPATION?

WHAT IS YOUR RACIAL/ETHNIC BACKGROUND?

WHAT ARE YOUR ASSETS?

FALSIFIED ANSWERS ARE CONSIDERED A PUNISHABLE CRIME.

THE ROMAN EMPIRE CENSUS BUREAU

We can't afford to lose more to Caesar's coffers.
They're taking food out of our babies' mouths
to feed their war machine. I won't let my labor be used
to fuel Roman public works projects.
What if we refuse to report? What do you think they'll do?
Drag us into the courts? Deport us from our fields
and seize our sheep? No chance.
They know they need us. But it's a risk.

SŌTĒR

Luke 2:11

I've heard it before.
We will rise up.
We will rage
against the machine
that crushes us

and we will do the
crushing. We will
grind them to
nothing. We will
be restored to our

former glory. I've
heard it before and
yet here we are. Still.
Our knives are no
match for their

swords. I swore
to myself I wouldn't
believe the hype
again. But here I am.
Wanting to believe it.
Wanting to hope.

When they keep snaking
ropes around our necks
and lifting us up as food
for the crows, I see no
other option than to throw
myself into this revolution.

....

Treasures

Luke 2:17-19

Some things that come my way
I take and quickly discard
so that they do not
wound and leave scars.

Or at least I try,
but these things somehow
burrow themselves deep
within my memories.

But other things uttered
by the tongues of those
who tend herds
of tender words

I hold close to my breast
and lock inside this treasure chest
so that bandits who ride by
cannot break inside and

steal my dreams. These
I ponder in the night watches,
praying they do not float away
on the winds of despair.

Ceremonies and Rituals

Luke 2:21-24

Yes, this is our duty,
but, oh, so much more.
This is who we are.

And we will not be erased.

We will name.
We will ritualize.
We will ceremonialize.
We will worship.
We will celebrate.

And we will not be erased.

This is part of our existence.
This is part of our resistance.
This is part of our faith.

And we will not be erased.

PROVISIONS

Luke 2:24

Momma always told me
that the Lord would make
provisions. She would
always put the *s* on the end.

But then I would watch them
in their fancy robes, and they'd
turn me away 'cause my clothes
had holes. Provisions? Seemed
to me like the Lord preferred
these divisions.

Us poor. Them not.
But what I never got
is why we waste time fighting
over the same small pot.

But, whatever. Provisions.
I need to live. And I need
to worship freely. I'm just
trying to maintain my dignity.

And so I sit here, lonely
on this bench. Actually,
I'm kept company
by these two pigeons,
and with their song they tell me
the Lord will make provisions.

We Gon' Be Alright

Luke 2:25-35

It's been a long time comin'.
I don't know how many years
and days I've been waitin' for
change. I've been playin'
Sam's song for far too long,
but I'm still holdin' on.

I saw a young man today. Not
even a young man, a baby boy.
And in that baby's cries I heard
rise the voices of future generations
singin' their song
that went somethin' like:

We gon' be alright!

And I believe it
because I have seen it.

GRAY HEADS

Luke 2:36-38

Where I'm from, you listen when the elders speak. I was taught early on that wisdom flows from gray heads. Respect. So when she approaches, I lend my ear. Bending over to hear because her back is bent low. That's years of carrying the heavy loads of our people's hopes on her broad shoulders. She's one of our matriarchs. Some call her church mother. This prayer bench, this wailing wall is well acquainted with her tears.

She speaks.   I listen.

Intently. Her voice trembles. Ever so gently. But her words are packed with the sort of power that opens heaven and shakes earth. Trust me, five minutes with her is well worth your time. The empire wants to discard her, widowed as she is, but around here she is held in high regard. She wants to prophesy over this child of mine, and I would be a fool to say no. Please. Let the wise words roll like honey off your aged lips. Whisper. I'll listen.

As Children Do

Luke 2:39-52

The dust from this gravel street
kicked up into the air from the feet
of children running, as they do.

As they do this on the gravel street
they kick up dust and play double-
dutch until evening rolls in.

Evening rolls in and I can't find the
child who loves to play in the gravel
street and kick up the dusty trail.

Up the dusty trail I travel to find him.
What's gotten into him?
What's he gotten into? As children do.

As children do, they surprise you. Their
wide eyes full of wonder and curiosity. They
are closer to heaven than we will ever be.

We will ever be learning from the children.
Learning from this child. Becoming like this child,
who has always known the way home.

III

IMMERSIONS

Alert to the Times

Luke 3:1-2

Wake up! The hardest work is to keep
from being lulled to sleep. To resist the
glazing over of my eyes and to stay alert
to the times. These are tyrannical days.
Power is used in diabolical ways. Displays
of allegiance will keep them off my back,
but they will remain on our necks.
So, what's next? This is a game of loyalty.
Who will I be in this moment of history?

Waters of
Insurrection

Luke 3:2-14

Never forget that justice is what
love looks like in public.
Cornel West

I went out into the desert
where the prophet speaks his word.
He spoke of things I cannot say
that I had ever heard.

His mouth was filled with power.
His eyes burned deep with fire.
But not because he hated,
it was justice he desired.

He wanted public love to roll
like fast and mighty rivers.
The things he said, they touched my core
and gave my soul a shiver.

I stood and listened closely
to hear him talk oppression,
but I could little understand
his talk about confession.

I came to hear him speak about
the sins of evil Rome,
but what he wanted was for me
to think upon my own.

Apparently, from what he says
my sins make me complicit.
He told me that repentance
is my real act of resistance.

He stood knee-deep in water
and reached in my direction.
I grabbed his hand and I stepped in,
committing insurrection.

TRADITION

Luke 3:4-6

We pass down this tradition
    like collard greens and
        black-eyed peas.

It's in mouths and
    bones and blood—
        it runs through our veins.

From the Euphrates to the Nile,
    past Jericho (shouts to Mr. Brown),
        to the Jordan and Mississippi.

It grows deep
    in our souls
        like the rivers.

From the year of King Uzziah
    to August 1963, this thing we call
        prophetic moves with kinetic energy.

Enough to flatten mountains
    and lift up valleys beneath
        our feet so we can be free.

But until we all taste this
    we will keep on passing down
        tradition to even out rough places.

Down by the Riverside

Luke 3:10-14

Look who came
to lay their burdens
down by the riverside!

The burdens of cheating us
and beating us until we bleed
are too heavy to bear.

Are my eyes deceived?
Do I really see officers,
soldiers, and the ones who

make us shoulder
heavy tax burdens?
I'm certain this is a revolution.

Nothing else would
make them respond to
rebukes with repentance

instead of
armoring up
with shields and defenses.

IMMERSION

Luke 3:15-18

I come up out of the water,
but I'm not done being immersed.

Submerged into the burning.
Plunged into the fire of the holy.

Wholly consumed, but not burned up.
A common bush enkindled with Spirit.

Sometimes I think about that bush
hiding up there on the mountain,

beckoning Moses to come and
warm his hands by the fires of justice.

Did it burn with fire
only when eyes turned in its direction?

Or did it possess a constant glow
even in the shadows of obscurity?

Good Trouble

Luke 3:19-20

Your voice
will get you
in good trouble

when you use it
to disrupt
the status quo,

when you raise it
to disturb
the false peace.

*Go get yourself
in some good,
necessary trouble.*

The Waters of
My Weeping

Luke 3:20

One of my brothers, my cousins,
added to the number of your incarcerated masses.
1 in 3 of us. Unarmed? Yes. A threat? Yes—
to your abuse of power, and the way you sit
so comfortably in your palace, while we struggle
to eat out in these streets.

But in this hour, I weep. Again.
For this innocent man baptized
into your carceral system. Immersed
into this jail with no bail.
I am forced to witness this unholy sacrament.
This state-sponsored religious act.
And for what? Something about his person
disturbed you. Maybe by passing him through
these waters you will convert him to the faith
of unsacred silence. One way or another.

I'm sorry that it frightens you when we
fight for our humanity. But tonight, I cry.
These tears have become my food. I dip
myself in the pool of the waters of my
weeping. For my brother. For my cousin.
For all of us. Until they stop locking us up.

ALL IN

Luke 3:21

Solidarity is a beautiful thing.
Jumping into the same waters
as sisters and brothers
is harder than I realized.

No performative show,
this is incarnation—
baptism into human skin.
This is what it looks like to be all in.

I AM SON

Luke 3:22

I've been called *son* before,
like I am something beneath
meant to be under someone.

Somewhere in my not-so-distant past
I was looked at as a boy,
but I'm a grown man.

And I understand what you mean
when you *son* me; my being is equal
to yours yet you still underfund me.

But run and tell that, I am *son*!
Running through these veins is Divine blood.
No matter what you call me you can't diminish royalty.

You might push me to the ground,
but I've got crowns
and I'm surrounded by glory.

There's only one Voice that
can tell me who I am.
Understand, I am *son*—a beloved one.

OF EARTH AND SKY

Luke 3:23-38

Let me tell you about the ancestors,
she said to me as I sat and relaxed
myself into Grandma's lap. She was
sharp, and even in her old age
her memory could search
into the far reaches of the past.

I can't stay up too late, not like I used to.
And then she proceeded to tell me tales
of Greats and Great Greats who did some
great and not-so-great things. Our family
tree is filled with triumph and struggle.
The imperfections make it beautiful.

They're all just human, you know, just like you.
She poked her frail finger into the flesh of my pectoral.
My kin, of the earth—the humus—yet filled with the breath
of God. Is this not what it means to be *adam*?

Never forget who you come from,
she said before calling it a night. Her words
implied that this sort of remembrance
would keep me grounded, but also keep me going.
Soaring high when they try to keep me down.
I won't forget that I am of earth and sky.

IV

TEMPTATIONS

DESERT OF DESIRE

Luke 4:1-3

And here he comes,
right on cue,
the one the folks used
to call Ole' Slew Foot.

This evil that slithers
between the feet of
Pharaohs and Caesars,
tempting me to be like them.

But such is common
to humanity,
and so it is here that
I must begin.

In this desert of desire.
In the badlands with
the bad man that
we all must battle.

This is the snake
that makes
empires great
again and again.

The time has come
for me to get bruised
while I crush him
under my foot.

Prove It

Luke 4:3-4

There is not a place in this world where I am not asked to prove it.
Substantiate my belonging.
Verify that my body is qualified to occupy this space,
as if the miracle of my enfleshment weren't enough.
But I am asked to be superhuman. Divine even. More than mediocre,
like the rest of them,
to demonstrate that my placement on this earth is not the mere result
of affirmative action.
But I will not eat the bread of your cunning. My sustenance is
found elsewhere.

VIEWS

Luke 4:5-8

The view from up here is beautiful.

> *There's nothing like a penthouse*
> *with a private rooftop deck to look*
> *out on all you have conquered—*
> *I mean, to look out at the city.*

This unobstructed view.

> *You can see from sea to shining sea,*
> *from the East River to the Hudson.*

It makes me want more.

> *And you can have it. Imagine the development*
> *you could do. We've already flattened Mannahatta,*
> *gave it a better-sounding name, and cleared out*
> *Seneca for our premier park. Let the horizon*
> *be your motivation. You only have to invest*
> *the small sum of your soul. And your people.*

You're selling this thing real good,
but I'll pass. That price is too high for my liking.

Shuckin' and Jivin'

Luke 4:9-12

Go on! Dance for me!
Move those feet! Shuck and jive
like I know you can. Go on! Dance!

Fancy me with your
smooth moves. Impress me with
your tricks. Do some flips and splits!

That will get you what you want.
The people will *ooo* and *ahhh*.
We'll all give you a round of applause.

Trust me. Do these things
and your name will be known. And them
pockets, watch how them pockets will grow.

I am not your prop.
I am not here to entertain.
And I refuse to play this little game of yours.

I know I have skills,
but don't try and twist this and
use it to line your pockets.

I will not be used.
You can't throw me a few dollars while
you continue to abuse my people. I'm no fool.

Don't test me!
I will not let you arrest me with your charm.
So like we say back home, get to steppin'!

An Opportune Time
(Out in These Streets)

Luke 4:13

I remember the day they gave me the talk:

Watch the way you walk,
out in these streets.

Pay attention to how you speak,
out in these streets.

In the car, try not to lean,
out in these streets.

No durag, keep yourself clean,
out in these streets.

You won't know at what moment,
out in these streets.

The man will be riding by,
out in these streets.

You gotta keep yourself ready,
out in these streets.

It will happen at an opportune time,
out in these streets.

THE ACCENT OF HOME

Luke 4:14-16

Returning home is always a conundrum.
Not because I don't love it, but because I love it.
It's a strange feeling to reenter the humdrum of
my former years that formed me. Riding by corners
where we used to act up. But since I packed my bags
and headed out, I'm not the same. It's not the same.

Maybe   change   is   good.

I wish they all could have come with me. All
these faces that I see in my night visions. How
will they respond to this new me? I feel like I vibe
with different energy these days. Honestly, if they
really knew me they'd know none of this is new.
Momma knows. This place will always be my place.
It grew me. Pop always told me *don't forget us when*
you make it big. I won't forget. I'll carry the accent of
home with me wherever I go. I just hope home doesn't
disown me.

4 × 100
(MY LEG OF THE RACE)

Luke 4:16-17

The baton has been passed,

                not

                        dropped.

A clean handoff. So I grab it and go.
Ready to run my leg in this relay.
I stand on the shoulders of those who
have run before. I am no rogue agent.

The

               path
has

               been
cleared.

It's my time. I continue the race of
those who have run against the grain
to lead us to a better way. I will spend
my days and work my legs to pass
this off to all of humanity—the anchor leg.

But I must put the team in position to
succeed. To follow through on what
we've been asked to do. This is faithfulness.
Who I am is not separate from the whole.
Ubuntu. Watch me run as I grab this scroll.
Let's roll.

THE ANOINTING

Luke 4:18

There are times when that something comes over you. You know those times. Pay attention. Let it fill you to overflowing. Allow it to move your pen to write. Open your mouth to say those words, at which you tremble. Pick up that brush to paint. Or sweep. But whatever that something moves you to do, let the Spirit take you.

To shake the foundations and make new worlds.
To break open new paradigms and design an unforeseen story.
To love. It will always move you to love.

When it comes it will drip slowly. Like oil. Running down the crown of your head, leaving little droplets of sweet-smelling perfume in the dust around you. Don't wipe your brow. Let it fall. The place on which you stand is holy ground.

Sometimes that genius will find you in the midnight hour. Other times it will overtake you at the high point of the day when all eyes are on you. No matter. The time will always be right. I have learned not to be surprised that I've been chosen. We have all been chosen for love. The anointing was given at creation's dawn. The oil always drips. Waiting for you, and for me, to stand under its flow.

BACK PEW TALK

Luke 4:18

Their good news ain't never been heard like that around here. What's good for them sounds like hell in my ear. You hear them cheerin? Four more years of their man. You know what that means for us? Nothin changin. Same ol same ol. Domination. Brutality. Low salary. We know what they mean when they say law and order. I heard that man Tutu said that good news to a hungry person is bread. What about if I'm just straight broke? I need that bread. And then preacher man gonna stand up here and tell us to wait until the sweet by and by. That's what he says all the time. I'm tired of this. We need something different. But different ain't never gonna come as long as we live under them. With their foot on our necks. I don't even know why I keep coming. I mean, I guess it's good to show face in this small town, but I'm not buyin what they're sellin. If I'm honest, though, I think I'm still hoping to snatch some kind of good news up in this place. That's why I sit here in the back. Only news they've got for me out there is some garbage about some bootstraps. Truth is, if it ain't good for us, it ain't good for no one. I need to hear some news that's good from the bottom up.

Euangelion (From Below)

Luke 4:18

Mother Fannie told me that I'm not free until you are too.

Brother James told me that this news gives me the courage
to break the conditions of servitude.

Now that's good.

I heard Brother Oscar say that this gospel must unsettle and shake.

Otherwise it's fake.

And Brother Gustavo maintained that the nature of this God is
to liberate.

Save me! Save us! Turn things right-side up! We've been on the
bottom. On the edges. Underneath.

Anawim.

Jubilee! A whole freedom! How foolish would I be to believe a word
that is satisfied with my chains?

This kind of news refuses to maintain the status quo.

This right here
is the gospel
from below.

Teaching Time

Luke 4:20

Mom used to sit.
Sometimes in her chair on the back deck,
sometimes on the edge of her bed,
but whenever she sat and called me,
I knew what time it had to be.

This was teaching time.
This was when I sat at her feet—my rabbi.
My eyes locked, my ears fixed
on the words that dripped
from her fountain of wisdom.
Whenever she sat, it was time to listen.
I knew I would not want to miss
whatever came next.

TODAY

Luke 4:21

I love today
as opposed to tomorrow.
Today is tangible.
Something I can hold
within my hands
and handle.

Tomorrow is always
an elusive illusion.
It is always future.
Something out there
that I am grasping at, but
for me, tomorrow is also easier.

It demands little of me,
unlike today,
which requires that I wake up,
put on my clothes, and go.
It shouts to me that I must show up.
I don't have to wait on it,
like tomorrow,
but I must be its servant.

Tomorrow lets me relax
and kick back.
But hey, there is never a moment
when it is not today.

CHALLENGE

Luke 4:22-30

There's a difference between
criticism and challenge,
although it's often difficult to
distinguish between the two.

Defenses. Put up the fences
when your words come for me.
Whatever your intention might be.

> *I don't like your tone.*
> *Who do you think you are*
> *coming home and talking like that?*
> *You went away for a few,*
> *now you're back acting all brand new.*
> *I don't know what it is you're talking about,*
> *but you're starting to sound like a sellout.*

Challenge is invitation.
Criticism turns my gaze upon your flaws
without a path forward. Call out,
but no call in. It's all love,
but to convince you of that is the hardest task.

APPARENTLY

Luke 4:25-28

My enemies.
Apparently,
God cares
for them
too.

Apparently,
salvation is
not just
mine,

but also
resides
on that
side of
the line.

Apparently,
that's supposed
to be
good news.

You could
have fooled
me.

Vengeance is
mine. I will
repay. Stay
away from
them with
Your mercy.

A RUDE AWAKENING

Luke 4:24-27

when you are finally
roused out of the dream world
in which God is only for you and yours
it will be a rude awakening

when you come to the realization
that God has always been for *them*
whoever *them* is
you will hear the sound of chains breaking

On the Edge of Things

Luke 4:29-30

I like to live life on the edge of things.
On that thin ledge where those who love most deeply find themselves,

teetering between being completely overwhelmed and absolutely
    obliterated.
The sort of love that is not afraid to say hard things always takes you to
    the brink.

It is not yet time for love to be my demise, but the path ahead is clear.
Soon enough I will be pushed off this cliff

                              falling

                          head

                      over

                  heels

              for

          my

      people.

POSSESSED

Luke 4:31-35

they showed up,
   unannounced,
      and stuck around.

moved in,
   set up shop
      in sacred places.

temples, bodies,
   and I don't know
      what to do. hell

has invaded
   what heaven
      created. I am

in turmoil,
   tormented by
      these forces

that signed a permit
   and built a high rise
      inside my mind.

. . .

on corners with
   big spotlights
      in my neighborhood

they sit and sit
    and harass me,
        especially at night,

time and time again,
    and I can't seem
        to get rid of them.

they cuff me,
    detain my mental space.
        seized by this evil

that sends me
    into seizures,
        convulsing for freedom.

AUTHORITY AND POWER

Luke 4:35-36

As a kid I learned rhymes
about sticks and stones.
I've broken a few bones in my time,
others' and mine.

My tongue is a minefield.
Watch your step or you'll get this work.
That's power. *Dunamis.*
Authority.

It was foreign to me
that I could use turn of phrase
to do the opposite
of devastate.

A new kind of power—
beautiful dynamism
that builds and heals.
What kind of word is this?

THE HOMES OF
MY FRIENDS

Luke 4:38-39

Growing up, sometimes I would
go to the homes of my friends and
their mothers would ask me to fix
some hinge on a door or mend the
leg of a broken stool. *Can you
bring your tools* they'd ask, usually
with a bit of laughter in their voices.
The way my father taught me to work
with timber was something special.
Nowadays, though,
I carry a different set of tools
with me wherever I go, but the requests
of my friends are still the same: fix this,
mend that, for my mother. And I'm always
glad to put to use what my Father taught me.
And the responses of the mothers of my friends
was always the same, they would thank me
and say *stay a while, let me put some meat
on those bones.*

N'EM

Luke 4:40-41

You know what happens when you make it.
When your name becomes commonplace in homes and on street corners.
They all come out the woodworks:
 aunties and uncles and cousins n'em.
And them "friends," in heavy quotes, that you haven't talked to since
    high school.
Then there's that person who knows a person who knows you.
It's cool. I'll do what I can. I love my people.

Desert Places

Luke 4:42

I have been given walls—
boundaries for my being.
It is sin to transgress the
limits that I was meant to
live inside. I am not
limitless. Holy it is to
embrace the limitations
that were placed on me
at creation. Displayed for
me on the seventh day.

Shabbat.

I will desert this city of demands
for a short while. Pitch my tent
among the mountains of my mind.
Climbing to these peaks so I can
see far above the chaos. Retreating
into this inner monastery. I must
leave in order to remain human, or
I will be ruined.

VOCATIO

Luke 4:43

I've wondered what I was made for.
I spent the years of my youth in my Father's house
reflecting out loud about this,

discovering my mission in this one fierce life.
For what purpose were the cells that make up this brown body
assembled on planet earth?

Was I sent to spend my days
proving to you that my existence matters?
Or is there more?

Maybe that is the more.
What could exceed the importance of binding humanity to humanity.
To the birds. The land. The trees. To Divinity.

My vocation
has been coded on strands of nucleic acid
since days long past.

Alas, this is why I passed
through the birth canal of the offspring of Eve:
to release justice, love, and shalom

into the atmosphere
of this blue and green spherical object
that I call home.

V

ROLLING DEEP

GENNESARET

Luke 5:1-3

it's calm at this time of day,
    usually. rays gently reflecting off
the shallow crests.

wind winding through
    the curls of my woolly hair.
piscine air

wrapping itself
    around me like we have
known each other

since beginnings.
    off this lake that
others call sea,

sound carries,
    blessing, interrupting
this momentary silence

with voices of
    beautiful beings approaching.
wanting more words.

BLUE COLLAR

Luke 5:3-5

We make livings.
Nothing extravagant—
far from it—
just what the fish bring in.

Blue collar
on this cerulean sea.
Trying to catch dollars,
what we call denarii.

There are days
when the nets
catch nothing.
This catch

nets nothing,
but food still
must find its way
to tables,

and taxes
must still
somehow land
in Roman hands.

Uncle Sam
always dipping
into my
little check.

I have next
to nothing left.
No product.
No plan.

Just this man
who I met
recently.
Some preacher

trying to
tell me
how to do
my job.

Jackpot

Luke 5:4-7

I always used to snicker, under my breath, at the people
lined up at the Shell station to purchase their Powerball tickets.
You could always tell them. They left their fingernails, at least one,
slightly long so that the scratch-off would be easy.

I don't believe in luck, at least not for us. We don't get lucky.
We get the scraps. Leftovers. Hand-me-downs. And they expect us
to be grateful. *Beggars can't be choosers.* Our lot in life was chosen
generations ago. We've been standing in this line for centuries.

Fingers crossed, hoping the ball bounces our way. Maybe someday it will.
Perhaps it will be today. I've got nothing to lose. I'll row out deep and
    take a leap of faith.
I'll cast these lots. Let the chips fall where they may. I still don't believe
    in luck,
but I do believe in favor. So much grace in this world you'll never be
    able to haul it all in.
Sometimes you just need to toss the net out again.

Few and Far Between

Luke 5:8

I   can't   find

        the   right   words
to   verbalize   what   I
    feel.   My   tongue   has   missed

    the   mark   of   utilizing
the   art   of   speech   but   as   I
traverse   through   this   linguistic

    abyss

    I   locate   these:

get away from me.

VOCATION: REDEFINED

Luke 5:10-11

I thought I knew
from day one—
this is what those
sons of Jonah do.

More than obligation,
this is honor.
Shame on me
if I turn my back

on family. Business
that builds a life
for us, but the pull
I feel to follow

another path is strong.
Magnetic, his voice is.
I dream of something
more for the first time.

How can I ignore
what the soul wants?
This must be what
destiny looks like.

Destined to catch
others in this net
of wild and wide
imagination.

What Love Touches

Luke 5:12-15

Touch. Skin on skin. Language of lovers.
And those who have known love.
Eros. Storge. Philia. Agape.
Alien tongue to me.

Toward me he reached, moving his lips in untypical ways.
I do want to were the words that formed
in his mouth and found their way
into my auricle.

Untouchable aura, which to me meant unlovable.
I have forgotten the shape of a hug.
I have lost faith that love exists.
This can't be real,

but there is nothing more real than feeling.
Hand gripping hand. Unafraid of
contamination. Love cannot
be made unclean.

No matter whom it touches.

WITHDRAW

Luke 5:16

My God, I withdraw
    so that I might be drawn closer,
        that nothing may hinder this flux of love.

This arid place
    deprives me of the praise
        that attempts to water my soul.

No applause
    from the hands of mortals,
        no lauding from their lips

can satisfy
    like the silence
        of this moment. With You,

O sacred silence!
    O saintly stillness!
        O solemn solitude!

Taking space
    to feel the air
        passing through pulmonary pathways.

Remaining connected
    to this holy ground
        beneath my feet.

Keep me grounded
    that I may not be found
        with hubris, forgetting

that I am
    ever of
        this humus.

CROWDED OUT

Luke 5:17-19

To be on the edge of the edge.
The bottom of the bottom.
Crowded out by the masses
trying to get their crumb.

Access is power. I'm rendered powerless
by my lack of it. Paralysis. My body won't even
allow me to push and shove. Legs won't budge.
These nerves will not receive cerebral signals,
but I am more than my condition.

Though we've been conditioned to believe
otherwise. I am not able to be human
in others' eyes. No ramps anywhere. I stare
at the backs of those gathered here.

THE CREW

Luke 5:17-19

How many of us have them?
The kind that ride or die,
side by side.

They move with me even when
I can't stand on my own two—
they carry me.
Bury hatchets

instead of catching grudges and clenching.
This bond is too important.
They are for me and
only for my good.

I would not be here, staring into hope's eyes,
if not for my crew that lifted me high
on faith-filled shoulders,
determined to see me rise.

WHO CAN FORGIVE

For The Charleston 9 and Botham Jean

Luke 5:20-21

who can forgive
a white man
walking into our Mother
to shoot the roofs off black bodies

who can forgive
a white woman
amber lite hair plain clothes wrong home
sending bullets through a brother

who can forgive
sins except
God
alone

Rise Up, My People!

Luke 5:24-26

Rise up!
Rise up, my people!
It's time to shake the dust.
It's time to claim your dignity.
Enough has been
enough!

Rise up!
Rise up, my people!
And live in shame no more.
Go strut into the future light.
There's greatness that's
in store

Rise up!
Rise up, my people!
And lift your voices high.
Let's sing the song that freedom brings.
Our sound will
never die

Rise up!
Rise up, my people!
Go on and talk that talk.
Put swagger in your step today.
It's time to rise
and walk!

INTERNAL DIALOGUE
AT A TAX BOOTH

Luke 5:27

I have made choices in life
of which I am not proud.
Haven't you?

You look at me as though
your rap sheet is
pristine.

Your eyes gleam with a
faux innocence which,
otherwise,

could be called guilt. I
struggle with that too.
I hate me

as much as you do.
If this is the price
I must pay

for survival then it is
not too high. I am
not the problem.

The society that has
set up these con-
ditions is.

Don't dish out your anger
on me. I'm just trying
to feed my kids.

Every choice in life is part
of a larger story.
What's yours?

Take the time to ask me
about mine before you
jump to your conclusions.

FOLLOW ME

Luke 5:27-28

Turn and leave your life behind.
More beautiful words have never been spoken.
My passage through seconds, minutes, and hours
could hardly be called life. Enticing.
Those words waft toward me like smells from Mom's kitchen.
They drift toward me supremely, like the love from Coltrane's saxophone.
I realize that those words, *follow me*, are just an invitation back home.

DINNER PARTY

Luke 5:27-31

Clink! Clink!
Turn down the music a little.
Let me say a few words as the host.
A toast! To our dear friend who put this evening together.
This spread is amazing!
I'm not even talking about the dinner,
this collection of sinners is splendid!
This is my kind of heaven.
A curator of souls, you are. The most eclectic kind!
Take a look around. Simply Divine!
We are the ones who have longed to be filled.
Others were invited, am I right, friend? But they said that their hunger
    was nil.
Their loss. So eat your fill, ladies and gents!
Our friend has promised that there is more where this came from.
The night is young. The party has barely begun!
Cheers to you! Mazel Tov!

Around Tables

Luke 5:29-30

We share identity. You identify with me. Though we are told we should not share space, the plates we pass preach solidarity.

This is where we plant our flag—on the continent of joy. We will not be removed from our native land, evicted from our house of ebullient jubilation.

Gifts are brought to this altar. Bread and wine. Stories and laughter. Fears and hope-laced tears. Presence is the greatest offering we can bring here.

We present our bodies, the dedication of our full selves to this moment. The foam that rises when a glass is poured tells us there is no need to rush. Settle in.

We give advice and shun the advice given. We take what we like and leave what we don't. Regardless, it's all love.

We ask about how days have been spent, and get upset when responses are curt. Clearly, there have been a few rough ones.

We pray and bless. Sometimes we curse. Pardon our unrefined speech.

We pass peace to each other, and share pieces of ourselves that would have remained tucked away had we not sat down.

We partake in our future destiny, as we break this bread and pass this cup, and dish out portions of this thinly sliced lamb. We always eat family-style.

WINESKINS

Luke 5:33-39

I have tried to fit the former
into the novel. It is fiction
to believe it is possible
to bring what once was
into what is becoming

or to place what is just blossoming
inside of what has already expanded
and has no stretch left. What is growing
cannot be confined. Some minds are rigid.
No give. They can only take so much

before they break. Opening is hard,
especially when it has been sealed
shut for some time. Realize it is a waste
of energy to try and reverse engineer
this process.

The new is lost when I try to preserve
the old. Some things just need to
be let go. What is coming needs room
to happen. To have an organic reaction. The new doesn't
need me to do its thing. It just needs space to breathe.

VI

On the Plain

FIELDS OF WHEAT

Luke 6:1

The beauty of Earth's golden hair
bent ever so softly by this breeze,
which offers the slightest relief from
the heat of the sun's rays.

There's nothing like the feel of
this tow-colored grass running
through my coarse hands. I feel
a kinship with this land.

A covenantal connection, as it was
always meant to be. We feed each
other. May this mutuality, this pleasant
interdependence, never be broken.

Sabbath

Luke 6:1-5

There is a realm of time where the goal is
not to have but to be,
not to own but to give,
not to control but to share,
not to subdue but to be in accord.

Rabbi Heschel

This sanctuary in time offers us the gift of return.
It beckons us back to our genesis,
where being human is all we seek to accomplish.
It was given, not for us to serve it, but to serve us—
a fountain of grace where we can remember
that we are not our labor,
that our true vocation is the double love of God and neighbor.
It is a day for reorientation and recalibration,
where celebration takes center stage.
On this day we renew our connection
with the community of all that has been made,
and with the Maker of all created things.

SAME ENERGY

Luke 6:1-11

Put me in jail, then.
Throw me behind your religious bars
since you have dubbed me a breaker of your law.

I live my days in the courtroom of your criticism.
I move unbothered under the gaze of your gavel.
I have no interest in defending myself before your bench.

Go on, clench your fists, raise your voice to make your point.
Type the rebuke that you must make on my page.
Who asked you to come through anyway? Is this rage your duty?

We operate under a different set of obligations,
and get worked up to frustration for different reasons,
even though we both claim fidelity to God.

If you were interested,
which I doubt,
here is where my passion lies:

feed the hungry,
clothe the naked,
heal the sick,

defend the rights of the orphan,
plead the widow's cause,
and woe to you who unjustly enforce God's Law.

Why spend your energy policing me
when that same energy could be used to love, fiercely?
Justice, mercy, and humility. Go learn what this means.

....

A Grand Unfolding

Luke 6:12-16

A new chapter begins,
  turn this page,
 not because the story is
  changing,
 it is just progressing forward.

I sit up all night,
  late like a writer into those hours
   only God is awake,
  to choose which names will dot
  tomorrow's blank pages.

It is agony to choose.
  I hate decisions.
  I only do what
   I am told.
Listening tells me where
  I need to go.

As the soft orange blaze of dawn
  begins to break
   around the corner
   of my window shade,
 it is time for me to descend
  this mountain of struggle.

To let the ink fall,
  letting these characters know
   which roles they will play
  in this grand unfolding
   as old as time.

NICKNAMES

Luke 6:13-16

Around the way
we don't use government names.

    Pookie. Peanut. Peaches.
    Big Head. Lil Man. Skip.
    Ski. Ace. Juney. Boog. Rock.

That's what they call me.
It must be my straight talk, sharp tone, rough edges.
Each moniker is a mark of endearment.
A secret passcode.
You only call me this if you know me.

We earn these
from personality,
physical features,
notorious acts,
like badges.
I'm honored by
this neighborhood
nomenclature.

In our crew we had that one dude—
everyone has that one dude—
who was the bestower of all nicknames.
If you got one from him
you knew you were in.
Gatekeeper.
There is no power like naming,
and I bear mine with pride.

HANDS FULL OF HEAVEN

Luke 6:20, 24

Hands held out.
The bottom edges pressed together,
making the shape of a metacarpus cup.

Nothing in them
except the air of aspiration,
anticipating grace from passersby.

I never miss
the gifts that heaven drops.
The crumbs from this table are decadent.

These people rushing by me
to arrive at their importance
miss so many riches.

Their hands
full of briefcases
and ambition.

I will take all the heaven
I can gather for today.
Tomorrow I will sit,

again,
with these hands cupped
to receive my enough.

LATE NIGHT
COMMERCIALS

Luke 6:21, 25

my eyes can't unsee
    rib cages. emaciated.
    bloated stomachs
    like balloons.
    late night commercials
       asking for a pledge
       to end world hunger,
       while I wipe chip grease,
       Lays, yellow bag,
       on my Nike sweats.
    I click past the sad music
    that sounds like angels weeping.
    my quick-twitching finger satisfies
    my appetite for apathy.
    blessed are those who hunger now.
tell me again what happiness is.

Fermented Lament

Luke 6:21, 25

Sadness has no place
in the land where the pursuit of happiness

is of first importance.
Declaring the gospel of independence

that has no sense of another's pain.
If only we could see that the notion of *the other*

is pure illusion.
Our suffering is one.

Then we would weep
instead of sweeping away the cries of generations.

Then we will laugh
as we sit around tables drinking the wine of our fermented lament.

Haters

Luke 6:22, 26

a proverb from the block:

> *if you have haters*
> *you're doing something*
> *right.*

and by right I mean living
as a conduit of Love.
let come the words
of those who feel exposed
by my spirit,
which insists on light.
it is an honor to be numbered
among the ancestors who
have been labeled as evil,
pegged as villainous,
agitators who pillage
the world for the loot of justice.
this is my heavenly reward.

> *if you have no haters,*
> *beware. you are probably*
> *in bed with mine.*

ENEMY LOVE

Luke 6:27

they came to our little town.
it was so quiet,
a silent night,

until they rode through
and took pieces
of our hearts.

slaughtered
our
innocents.

my chest pounded and
beads of sweat dribbled
down my temple

as I hid with him,
my infant, my boy,
cloaked underneath my prayer shawl.

but infants have not yet learned
the rules of our world:
to be quiet

to look down at the dirt and
hush your sound when
they are around.

his cry gave our hiding place
away and they
took him.

away from my arms he went
and then it was
a silent night again,

for a moment, until I
joined the chorus
of mothers
wailing under the cover
of now-empty
prayer shawls.

the shrill weeping
of that night
haunts me.

Turning Cheeks

Luke 6:29

His words sound sweet and docile,
but there's a reason he's treated as a hostile threat.
I would not be found in his company
if his goal was for me to be trampled like a doormat.

His talk of cheeks sounds meek and mild,
but I can see inside his strategy,
teaching us to subversively reclaim our dignity
by insisting that they see our humanity.

You will not backhand me.
I will not be treated as your underling.
You must look me in the eye and
slap me with the forehand side.

We are equal.

GRADE SCHOOL ETHICS

Luke 6:31-38

Back in grade school,
we were children.

We learned addition. We learned subtraction. We learned how to
act human.

    Treat others the way you want to be treated.
    You get back what you give out.

We wrote these words on ruled sheets of white paper with golden
number two pencils.

I was kind to the bullies.
I was still bullied.

I'm still waiting on the return for my investment. The world has a
tendency to short-change me.

                                              go high.
At home I learned that when the bullies   *we*

                        go low

Always be golden, aureate. The bullies win when you let them dim
your shine.

LOGS AND SPLINTERS

Luke 6:39-42

I look around
surveying the crowd, wondering
why
no one's paying attention.

Everyone distracted by
their cellular gadgets,
lost in a world that is not
here.

That girl over there,
running her fingers through
the grass like scissors,
parting that sea of green
with her phalangeal staff,
seems uninterested.

Just a little ways up from me
I see a man's head
rising and falling,
as if on a yo-yo string,
trying to pretend that he has not dozed off.

They don't understand the value
of these words.
Why are they even
here?

a bony elbow nudges my arm. A voice whispers

Did you hear that?
I need to sit with that one for a while.
Splinters? Logs? Wow.

Tell me once he's done.
I must have
missed
that part.

OUR GOOD TREE

Luke 6:43-45

Abba would head out early in the morning
to pick fresh figs from the tree in our yard.
The handcrafted stone bowl sitting in the
middle of the table, the one made by immah,
would hold those purplish-red jewels. Their
skin still warm from the summer sun. *They're*
best when they've just come off. I heard those
words countless days as my teeth pierced the
outside flesh. Abba used to call it our good tree.
Juice dribbling down my face from the corner of
my mouth. *That's how you know it's good—*
the way the fruit tastes when it hits your tongue.
On those early summer mornings I learned life lessons.
You never have to guess what a person is
all about. Just pay attention to the fruit. It never lies.

WISE WORDS
FROM MOM

Luke 6:46-49

Mom used to have this saying:

> *Don't tell me that you heard me,*
> *just do it.*

She usually said something
along these lines
after stepping over clothes of mine

in the room
she had asked me to clean
two days prior.

After trying to make my case to her
as to why my room still looked
like Gehenna,

she would look at me with those eyes
that only mothers can make
and say:

> *Don't be a fool.*
> *Do what I've asked you to do.*

I had no idea back then
that she was speaking
the wisdom of heaven.

VII

LIFE LESSONS

I STRUGGLE WITH THE WORD DESERVES

Luke 7:1-5

We grow apples here.
They are not famed like
the olive or the fig,
but they do exist.

The universal law of apples
applies to them,
as everywhere:
one bad apple.

I've been told
there are *good ones*
among the batch of golden-colored
with the brush of red across the top.

We call them centurion.
But how good can they be
if the whole tree is rotten
at the root?

I struggle with the word *deserves,*
as if decent behavior
inside a corrupt system
has earned a gold star.

What I am learning from him
is that all who possess flesh and blood
are *deserving* of love and dignity.
No matter the tree.

I still need some convincing,
but he claims
this is the way
the whole system will be undone.

UNDER THE RUBBLE

Luke 7:6-10

I learned, early on, that certain people
and places were God-forsaken.
Faces upon whom the Divine sun
does not shine.

> *The LORD be gracious*
> *to Us*
> *and bless*
> *Us.*

But my countenance fell
when he said that great faith
was found in their land.
Amongst their people.
Amidst that evil.

The greatest he had ever seen.
The force of that statement
felt like a bomb dropped
on the walled-in city of my life.

When your worldview explodes
and you are left under the rubble
of what was once fortification,

you can either work to emerge
into a new mystery
or suffocate under the pile
of your illusory certitude.

YOUTH MORTALITY

Luke 7:11-12

Is high.
An accepted fact of life
in Nain
and places like it.
Mothers
watching bodies
of once lively sons,
now draped in flowers,
prepared
for the ground.
To make it past
the tender ages
could only
be called
miraculous.

Mothers Like Us

Luke 7:13

These tears stream. For all mothers, everywhere, who know this pain.
Mammie. Lezley. Samaria. Sybrina. Tressa. Valerie (both of them). *Hawa.
Kadiatou. Constance. Iris. Larcenia* (weeping from the heavens as her
boy called for her), and the tens of thousands of others who have
known the feeling of being wordless. And sonless.

These tiny tunnels

behind my eyes

won't stop

their flooding.

Like the broken faucet

of my bathroom sink

there is no turning this off.

My hands are motionless, down at my side. Yet, somehow, I feel a
finger running gently underneath my right eye. Collecting my liquid
grief, while these words reach me:

Don't cry.

The words heaven speaks to the mothers of earth. Mothers like us.

Magic Words of Spring

Luke 7:14-15

We live in a world
where dead things return
to the land of the living.

A world of wonder,
an earth full of magic.
Every year spring happens.

His words are enchanted,
possibly necromancy.
Calling my dearly departed

to get up,
like he had simply chosen
to lay his head and make his bed

in the place
where dead sons wait
to hear the magic words of spring.

FROM BEHIND BARS

Luke 7:18-23

From behind bars it's hard
to see if the long arc
of the moral universe
is bending toward justice.

I have heard reports of a movement,
working to bring change,
but all I can see are COs and prison guards
laughing at talk of abolition.

And I laugh
to cover up the fact
that my hope is waning.
Little light remains in this dungeon.

Is this really you?
Is this really a God move?
Or should I just keep waiting
with the patience that killed the ancestors?

G.O.A.T. Status

Luke 7:24-30

Tell me,
how can it be
that a crazy,
seemingly deranged man
who wears camel hair
and flails about
in wild places
is worthy of
such high praise?

I raise
my eyebrows at
such a ludicrous notion—
the one who
shouted wrath and
made them take baths
in unsanitary rivers
could be given
such an unheard of
title like

Greatest human
Ever born.

Never.
He is criminal. Locked
in Herod's prison.
Hands and feet
in chains.

Perhaps his insistence
on change
is what makes him great.
And I
who remain content with
what is
am the problem.

Demonized

Luke 7:31-35

It does not seem to matter how we do this work:

> with bullhorns or ballpoint pens,
> with demure conversation or deafening protest,
> with justified rage or joyful resistance.

We will still, somehow, be demonized.

> Labeled as rabble-rousers.
> Agitators.
> Those who stand against the work of God in the world.

It seems to me
the issue is not our methods,
but that we would dare raise our voices
to challenge the status quo.

The problem is that we
have the audacity
to say *woe* to you.

What we do is madness.
We must be crazy
to believe that change could come
to this generation.

So go ahead and frame us.
Continue to blame us for disturbing your false peace.
Keep covering us in your lies.
We will prove to be the wise ones
in the eyes of history.

WHEN *THEY* INVITED ME FOR DINNER

Luke 7:36

Eating together
communicates
identification.
I recognize you
as human,
even when we
don't see eye to eye,
if there was any wonder
why I take my seat
at this table.

ALABASTER

Luke 7:37-39

Word got around
that the one who does wonders
is under their roof.
I wonder what he'll do for me.
Will he

> Reject me, as do the ones he eats with?
> Subject me to false perceptions?
> Accept me?

I guess acceptance is worth the risk
when you are constantly dismissed
by men who claim to be agents of God.

But despite what they say,
I know God.
And I have learned to discern the difference
between Pharisaical leaven
and bread from heaven.

My tears can't help but roll
when I taste sweet mercy,
when I am shown worth
instead of hurried out of his presence.

I break open the alabaster jar
of my one precious life
to pour out on the beautiful feet
of this one who brings good news.

THREE KINDS
OF SINNERS

Luke 7:39

There are three kinds of sinners in this world:

1. Those who know it

2. Those who don't

3. Those who don't care

The ones who know pour out perfume.
The others stand around judging
and wondering at such waste.

I Screen Calls

Luke 7:41-50

I try to avoid my phone
when unknown numbers
flash across my screen.

I screen calls.
If you're not locked in my contacts,
don't bother.

It's probably them debt collectors calling.
What I owe could fill two U-Hauls.
They're gonna haul me away.

Or at least take everything I've got.
I have no idea why I decided
to press that green button today.

But the voice I hear tells me
my debt has been canceled.
Probably a scam. I ask for answers.

I receive one: forgiveness.

VIII

PARABLES AND OTHER THINGS

AND MANY OTHERS

Luke 8:1-3

*Like a lot of Black women, I have always had
to invent the power my freedom requires.*
JUNE JORDAN

I will begin
by saying their names:

Mary of Magdala
Joanna
Susanna

They will not
become footnotes
on the pages
of this story.

They possess
no fancy moniker,
no honor given them
by men
claiming
theological acuity.

But they did own
the bag,
making it possible for
a ragtag group of guys
to get all the credit.

And many others,
sisters, aunties,
mothers, daughters,
unnamed, yet
undeterred
from the work
of freedom.

The Power of Parable

Luke 8:4

The destiny of Earthseed is to take root among the stars.
Octavia Butler, *The Parable of the Sower*

Down through the ages, we've passed down wisdom through story. This is what the scholars call oral tradition. We simply call it living, because there is no life without the elders gifting us their parabolic insight. Subversive, like Octavia's Earthseed. They unearth the power of our humanity that has been covered by years of subjugation, reminding us of our connection to the Divine. They tell us of things certain folks fear, things those on top do not want us to hear. So give ear when these stories are uttered. It is here that we must do battle, rattling the cages of evil with the power of parable.

OF SEEDS AND SOIL

Luke 8:5-8

I spent years on the farm with Saba, learning
the tricks of our family trade.
He taught me about seeds;
and as he would hold a tiny one between his thumb
and his pointer finger, I would linger on every word.

There are generations in this seed—
future life for those yet to be born.
The seed always has the potential for life,
but it is not a sole actor. There are other factors
that must align for the seed to unleash its full potential.
It must take up residence in hospitable soil,

which is why Saba always spent so much time
clearing the ground before laying down the seed.

Our celestial Brother Sun must lend his hand,
and ample rain must fall to nourish our arid land.

He taught me these things
so that I might pay attention,
and learn that the flourishing of life
is not independent,
but is interconnected,
part of a larger web that must come together.

You are part of the link, and if you have ears to hear
you will understand the rest in due season.

Mysteries

Luke 8:9-15

I have been told that
mystery is not what is unknowable,
but what can be infinitely known.
The fog remains
for those who refuse to search—
for those who walk away without explanation,
frustrated with the riddle of life.

MY LIGHT

Luke 8:16-18

Shine on all of them. My umi said to shine your light. . . .
You were born to win. Don't let them make you
colorblind and not adore your skin.

TOBE NWIGWE, "SHINE"

I learned the song
of my little light
way back in Sunday school

Bushels and all
and never hide
but keep the light in view

Now years have passed
and I still love
the truth of that sweet song

but now I gasp
at words of those
who made me sing along

My light
is not compliance
or quiet assimilation

My light
might be defiance
and righteous indignation

MY LIGHT

Luke 8:16-18

Shine on all of them. My umi said to shine your light. . . .
You were born to win. Don't let them make you
colorblind and not adore your skin.

TOBE NWIGWE, "SHINE"

I learned the song
of my little light
way back in Sunday school

Bushels and all
and never hide
but keep the light in view

Now years have passed
and I still love
the truth of that sweet song

but now I gasp
at words of those
who made me sing along

My light
is not compliance
or quiet assimilation

My light
might be defiance
and righteous indignation

My light
will not blend right in
and go with what's allowed

My light
might just put up a fight
scream and get real loud

My light
must never mask
cover or conceal

My light
takes up this task:
to bring the truth, unveil, reveal

This
little light
of mine

FAMILY

Luke 8:19-21

The nuclear one
that they've ripped up
and then called broken.

The one where
they separated fathers, mothers, daughters, sons,
from the auction block to gen pop.

But see, family
has always been much wider.
Divine in nature.

And those who love
are those who understand
what it is we are a part of.

We are keepers
of brothers and sisters.
We don't sell them or put them in cells.

This is the will of God
since the foundation
of the world. *Ujima.*

THE RAGING SEA

Luke 8:22-25

Growing up, I heard tales of sea monsters.
Some called them whales,
some said Leviathan—
giants,

the size of empires.
Untamable, chaotic, overwhelming.
No one could tell what
their next move would be.

We never stood a chance,
like minnows,
in the ocean of great powers.

The only thing more potent
than the monsters who cause storms
is the one who can calm them. But I guess
he's sleeping, because these beasts rage on.

Legion

Luke 8:26-39

I have seen Legion
in my region of the world.

Occupying forces
that distort my humanity.
Always waging war,
driving us to insanity.

Legion is many.
Enemy.
Supremacy.

Oppresses from the outside
and takes up residence inwardly.

Getting rid of this demonic dynamism
will upset the system,

but my wholeness
hinges
on its exorcism.

TESTIFY

Luke 8:39

First giving honor to God,
who is the head of my life.

Everyone knows this phrase
out where I'm from.
It's what we say when we testify
to what God has done.

You might hear a couple *mmmhmms,*
followed by a few *welllls.*
Don't let him grab the mic,
he's got a story to tell.

the B3 organ sounds

He picked me up!
Turned me around!
Placed my feet!
On solid ground!

When he came through my hood,
I finally understood
what we mean we say
God is good.

All the time.

Talitha

Luke 8:40-42

My little girl.
Technically,
she is
now old enough
in our culture
to be considered
grown,
but to me
she is still
Talitha.

As her abba
I am
obligated
to seek her
wellness
no matter what her
age is.

It has been
hell here
as she nears
death.

When you are
desperate,
proper etiquette
is sent
packing.

NEVER MAKE
YOURSELF SMALL

Luke 8:43-48

I was a little girl once.
I used to run free,
and I remember the day
my mother told me

> *Never make*
> *yourself small.*
> *You are a daughter*
> *of God.*

I was tall for my age.
My presence would
intimidate the boys.
I learned not to take up space.

And when my body
went through changes,
I stayed in the place
the boys made for me.

Shunned.
Unclean.
Forever
Unseen.

Today I must
sneak in
for my healing.
Keep being small.

When I reach out and touch,
he calls me by name:
Daughter,
and all mother's words return.

I am free
to stand tall again.

To Be a Realist

Luke 8:49-50

I am a realist.
I deal in the logical,
but sometimes reality
must give way to impossible.
Especially for the sake
of our children.

In the Room

Luke 8:51-53

When God has promised
to change what's been called
unchangeable,
to resurrect what has been
pronounced dead,
only those who believe
can be in the room
where it happens.

EAT YOUR FILL

Luke 8:54-56

Breath, returning.
Neurons, firing.
Eyes, widening.
Mouth, smiling.
Body, reviving.
Life is mine,
again.

Get up, my child,
and eat your fill.
Today is yours
for living.